A New True Book

MANATEES

By Emilie U. Lepthien

CHILDRENS PRESS®

CHICAGO

A manatee fountain greets
visitors to Tampa's Lowry Park.

PHOTO CREDITS

© Emilie Lepthien—2, 25 (left), 41 (top), 44 (2 photos)

North Wind Picture Archives—4 (bottom), 7 (left), 13

Photri—© D & I MacDonald, 42

Root Resources—© Doug Perrine, 7 (right), 10, 22, 23, 29 (right), 32, 35, 40 (left), 45

Tom Stack & Associates—© Jeff Foott, Cover, 9, 20 (right), 27 (left), 29 (left), 40 (right); © M. Timothy O'Keefe, 19, 41 (bottom); © Rod Allin, 20 (left)

© Lynn M. Stone—39 (left)

U.S. Fish and Wildlife Service—Sirenia Project—17 (right), 18, 21, 25 (right), 31

UPI/Bettmann—24 (right), 36

Valan—© Jean-Marie JRO, 4 (top); © Jeff Foott, 12, 15 (right), 17 (left), 24 (left), 27 (right), 28; © Stephen J. Krasemann, 15 (left); © Thomas Kitchin, 39 (right)

Cover—Manatee, Crystal River, Florida

Library of Congress Cataloging-in-Publication Data

Lepthien, Emilie U. (Emilie Utteg)
  Manatees / by Emilie U. Lepthien.
    p.   cm. — (A New true book)
  Includes index.
  Summary: Discusses the family history, habitat, appearance, infancy, behavior, and protection of this gentle, endangered sea mammal.
  ISBN 0-516-01114-6
    1. Manatees—Juvenile literature. [1. Manatees.]
I. Title.
QL737.S63L47   1991
599.5′5—dc20   90-21138
                                      CIP
                                      AC

TABLE OF CONTENTS

The statue of Hans Christian Andersen's Little Mermaid (above)
is in Copenhagen, Denmark. Mermaids, sea creatures of myth
and legend, are often shown in works of art (below).

MISTAKEN IDENTITY

For many years sailors told stories about sea sirens, or mermaids. They thought mermaids were half human, with a fish's tail instead of legs and feet. Sailors thought mermaids lured them onto treacherous rocks with their songs.

Christopher Columbus saw manatees in 1493 when he reached the New World. He thought they were mermaids.

In his log Columbus wrote: "They are not as beautiful as they are painted. To some extent they have a human appearance in the face."

Today people look at manatees and wonder how anyone could think they were mermaids. Perhaps sailors didn't get a close look at the manatees. Perhaps they just had good imaginations.

A manatee, swimming with a human friend at right, does not really look like the artist's idea of a sea siren, seen at left.

Manatees are marine, or aquatic, mammals. They belong to the order, or group, of animals called *Sirenia*. The name recalls the sailors' belief in mermaid sirens.

MANATEE SPECIES

There are three species of manatees—the West Indian manatee, the Amazon manatee, and the African manatee. They are all vegetarians. They eat plants growing in the shallow water along the coasts of oceans, in bays, and in rivers. The shallow water protects them from large predators living in deeper water. Manatees are gentle and harmless. They

A West Indian manatee swims in the Crystal River in Florida.

have no way to defend
themselves against
predators. They are also very
curious. All three manatee
species are now on the
endangered species list.

A manatee mother and calf

West Indian manatees are found along both coasts of Florida during the winter. In summer they migrate northward in the Atlantic Ocean as far as the Carolinas and Virginia. Some

move west along the Gulf
Coast as far as Louisiana
and Texas. They have been
found in coastal and inland
waters in Central and South
America as far south as
Recife, Brazil. There are only
about 1,200 West Indian
manatees in Florida waters.

The Amazon manatee
lives in the Amazon River in
South America. It is the only
manatee that lives only in
fresh water. The Amazon
manatee is hunted by

Manatees are fishlike in shape, and their bodies are almost hairless.

people living along the river. Manatee meat is a prized food. If hunting continues, this manatee species will become extinct.

The African manatee lives along the coast and in the inland waters of west central Africa. Scientists do not know much about this species.

A dugong has a split tail.

DUGONGS

A fourth animal in the order *Sirenia* is the dugong. Dugongs are much like manatees. They prefer the warm waters on the shores of Indian and Pacific Oceans. They are found from East Africa to northern Australia, in Indonesia, and north to the Philippines.

The Steller's sea cow was a species of dugong. It was discovered in the Bering Sea in 1741. This was the only *Sirenia* species that lived in cold waters.

Steller's sea cows were about 23 feet (7 meters) long. They weighed several tons. They were hunted to extinction in 1768, only 27 years after they were discovered.

Except for their thick, wrinkled skin, manatees (right) do not look much like their nearest relatives, the elephants (left).

LAND-DWELLING RELATIVES

The manatee is thought to have evolved from a four-footed land mammal that lived millions of years ago. Its nearest modern relative is the elephant. Manatees are not related to whales or dolphins.

15

WHERE DO MANATEES LIVE?

Manatees are marine animals. They live in fresh or salt water. They prefer shallow water where the temperature is over 68° F. (20° C).

During an unusually cold Florida winter, the temperature of the air may drop below 50° F. (10° C). If the water temperature drops below 68° F., the manatees are in trouble.

Manatees love to play.
Several are swimming
in this Florida river.

Manatees have a layer of
blubber under their thick
skin to protect them from the
cold. But they cannot survive
if the water temperature is
below 68° F. for several days.

Florida manatees gather in the warm water
from a power-station discharge point.

In Florida the discharge
water from power stations
keeps the temperature in
some rivers or estuaries at
72° F. (22° C). The manatees
gather in this warm water from
November through March.

WHAT DO MANATEES LOOK LIKE?

West Indian manatees are
a gray or gray-brown color.
They are shaped like large
fish or seals. Their bodies
taper toward the tail. Their

Manatees have no hind limbs or fins.

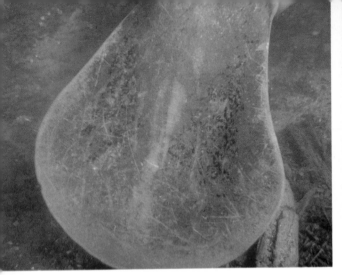

The manatee's rounded tail is paddle-shaped.
The one on the right has been tagged by scientists
who will follow its movements by radio.

tails are paddle-shaped,
with a rounded end. These
shy animals move slowly
through the water by
pumping their tails up and
down.

Adult male manatees may
be over 13 feet (4 meters)
long. They may weigh more
than 1,500 pounds (680

Manatees have "fingernails" at the ends of their flippers.

kilograms). They mate when they are five to nine years old. Adult females are somewhat smaller.

Manatees have two small forelimbs, or flippers. Each flipper has three or four claws like fingernails.

Manatees use their flippers
to steer while swimming.
They do not have hind limbs.
   A manatee's skin is thick
and wrinkled and almost
hairless. Individual manatees
can be identified by cuts that
have healed on their backs.
Boaters often ignore signs

The light marks on this manatee's side are
scars from wounds caused by power-boat propellers.

Many manatees have survived several run-ins
with boat propellers. Mutilations are common.

posted to limit speed in
manatee protection zones.
When power boats travel too
fast, their propellers can
cut into the manatees' skin.
The slow-moving manatees
cannot evade the boats.
Injured manatees may be
taken to marine animal
hospitals for treatment.

These pictures show the manatees' wrinkled skin
and the bristles around their mouth.

SPECIAL ADAPTATIONS

Manatees have pudgy faces.
The skin on their heads and
faces is wrinkled. There are stiff
hairs, or bristles, around the
snouts. These bristles help
them feel for plant food.

Their eyes are small. In

the water their eyes are covered with a thin skin, or membrane, to protect them.

Manatees can hear very well. On the top of their snouts, there are two small nostrils. These holes close tightly when they are under water. They open when the manatees surface to breathe.

A manatee (left) surfaces with its nostrils open. Manatees come to the surface to breathe every three to five minutes.

EATING, RESTING, PLAYING

Manatees spend from six to eight hours a day feeding. They eat submerged and floating plants. They eat 10 to 15 percent of their body weight each day.

The manatee's mouth is well adapted to feeding on the bottom. They push plants into their mouth with their flippers. They chew the plants with their strong molars. These teeth wear down as they chew the tough plant fibers. Their molars are constantly replaced, like an elephant's teeth. Both males and females have horny plates in their mouths to help them crush food.

Manatees eating water hyacinths

A manatee resting on the river bottom

These large aquatic animals never come ashore. Instead, they rest for two to twelve hours a day at the bottom or near the surface of the water. They come up to breathe every three to five minutes. They can remain underwater for longer periods when

they are just resting.

Manatees are generally
solitary animals. They often
play by themselves. They
swim on their backs, body-
surf, and roll over and over.

Since they have no natural
enemies, manatees do not need
the protection of a herd or a
large group. When they gather
in small groups, they do not
seem to have a leader.

COMMUNICATING

Divers have recorded the squeaks and squeals made by manatees. They make sounds when they are frightened or playing. The cows and calves also make sounds to communicate.

Sometimes when two manatees meet, they seem to "kiss" each other. Perhaps they are saying "Hello."

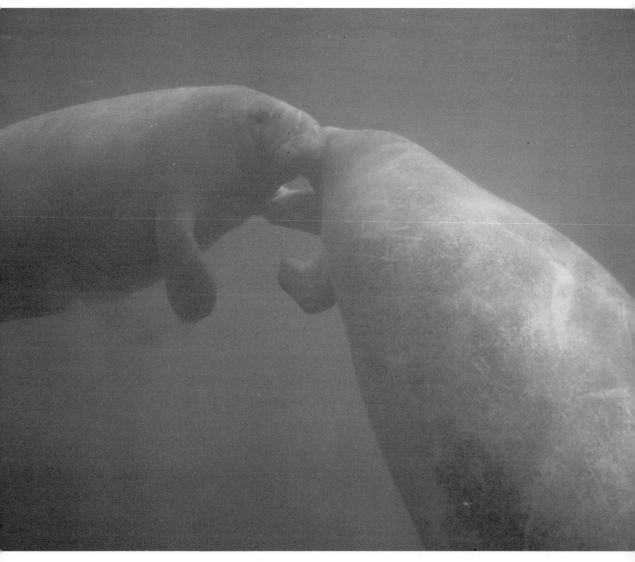

Manatees "kissing" as they meet

MANATEE CALVES

Like other mammals, female manatees give birth to live young. Usually manatee cows have just one calf. It is born underwater. Calves are born thirteen months after the cow has mated with a manatee bull.

Calves are 3 feet (1 meter) long when they are born. They weigh from 60 to 70 pounds (27 to 31 kilograms). Their skin at birth is almost black.

Opposite page: A manatee calf nursing. The mammary glands are high on the mother's chest, under the flippers.

Immediately after the calf is born, the mother brings it to the surface of the water. They both must breathe air. The mother may dunk the calf several times. This is how she teaches it to go under the water by itself. The calf nurses on its mother's milk underwater.

Calves may feed on mother's milk for two years. But they begin to eat aquatic

Sometimes manatees have twins.
This mother has two calves to care for.

plants a few weeks after they
are born.

Cows have a calf every two
or three years. The females
have full responsibility for
taking care of the calves. The
bulls do not help in any way.

Cows must be from five to

This manatee cow will soon give birth.

nine years old before they can mate. The low birth rate is one cause of the decline in the manatee population.

LIFE EXPECTANCY

Scientists are not sure how long manatees will live. Each year more than 100 manatees die in Florida waters. In 1989 a record number of 166 manatees died. One-third were killed by run-ins with power boats and barges. Many died following the Christmas freeze.

In 1982, there was an outbreak of "red tide" off southwest Florida. The red tide was caused by toxic, microscopic marine organisms. Manatees feeding in seagrass beds ate these toxic organisms. As a result, 37 manatees died.

Many manatee feeding grounds are lost when wetlands are destroyed. Pesticides and other chemicals wash into canals,

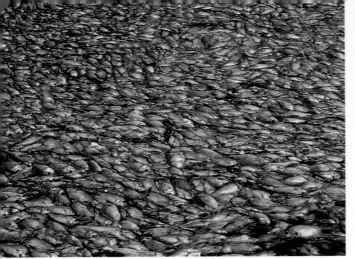

Fish (above) killed by a red tide. Chemical pollution (right) in marshes affects the food supply of animals that live there.

rivers, and drainage areas. These pollutants endanger manatees.

The garbage that people throw into the water can also endanger manatees, other marine life, and birds. Since manatees are very nosy and playful, they investigate

Left: The manatee on the right is scarred from being caught in a fisherman's crab trap. Right: A sign at Merritt Island Wildlife Refuge warns boaters to watch out for manatees.

discarded fishing lines and hooks. They can become entangled in the lines, in discarded nets, and other debris. Human carelessness has helped to put Florida's manatees on the endangered species list.

PROTECTING THE MANATEES

In 1978 the Florida Manatee Sanctuary Act was passed. The entire state was made a manatee sanctuary. From November 15 to March 31, boats must travel at very slow speeds in special areas where manatees gather. There are twenty-two such manatee protection zones in Florida.

Unfortunately, some boaters ignore these warning signs, and many manatees are injured or killed each year.

A scientist works with manatees at Nature World in Homosassa Springs, Florida.

At Homosassa Springs, nine manatees can be seen year-round. They are protected in the state park on the Homosassa River. Some electric power stations have built viewing platforms where visitors can watch the manatees swimming in the warm water that the plant discharges. Tampa Electric Company also provides manatee information to the public.

Schoolchildren (right) come to see
Snooty (above) at the South Florida Museum.
Snooty loves to show off his whiskers.

SNOOTY

More than forty years ago,
Snooty was born in captivity
in Miami. When he was young,
Snooty was moved to a large
tank in the South Florida
Museum and Bishop Planetarium
in Bradenton.

This nursing calf will soon be eating plants on its own.

Biologists come to the museum to study Snooty. Schoolchildren and adults learn a great deal about manatees when they visit Snooty. They learn how important it is to protect an endangered species in its natural habitat.

WORDS YOU SHOULD KNOW

aquatic (uh • KWAW • tik) — living in water

blubber (BLUH • ber) — fat that forms in a layer under the skin of manatees, seals, and other marine mammals

decline (dih • KLYNE) — to gradually get worse or become less in number; to decay

endangered (en • DAIN • jerd — in danger of dying out

estuaries (ES • choo • air • eez) — the wide mouths of rivers where the tide flows in

evolve (ee • VOLVE) — to gradually develop over the generations

extinct (ex • TINKT) — no longer living

fibers (FYE • berz) — tough, stringy plant tissues

habitat (HAB • ih • tat) — the place where an animal usually is found

life expectancy (LYFE ex • PEK • ten • see) — the number of years an animal can be expected to live before dying a natural death

marine (muh • REEN) — of the ocean

membrane (MEHM • brayn) — a thin, skinlike tissue

microscopic (my • kroh • SKAH • pik) — so small that it can only be seen with a microscope

migrate (MY • grayt) — to travel, usually for a long distance, to find more food or better weather conditions

molars (MOH • lerz — broad, flat teeth

nostrils (NAH • strilz) — openings in the nose through which air is taken in

organism (OR • gah • niz • em) — any living thing; a plant or an animal

pesticides (PESS • tih • sides) — chemicals that kill insects and other organisms that harm crops

pollutants (puh • LOO • tents) — chemicals or other materials that make the air or water dirty

predator (PREH • da • ter) — an animal that kills and eats other animals

sanctuary (SANK • choo • air • ee) — a place of safety; a place where animals are protected from their enemies

solitary (SAHL • ih • tair • ee) — living alone

species (SPEE • seez) — a group of plants or animals that are alike in certain ways

submerged (suhb • MERJD) — underwater

toxic (TAHX • ik) — harmful to living things

treacherous (TRECH • er • us) — not to be trusted; dangerous

vegetarian (veg • ih • TAIR • ee • an) — an animal that eats only plants

INDEX

About the Author

Emilie Utteg Lepthien earned a BS and MA Degree and certificate in school administration from Northwestern University. She taught third grade science and social studies, and was a supervisor and principal of Wicker Park School for twenty years.

   Mrs. Lepthien was awarded the American Educator's Medal by Freedoms Foundation. She is a member of Delta Kappa Gamma Society International, Illinois Women's Press Association, National Federation of Press Women, Iota Sigma Epsilon Journalism sorority, Chicago Principals Association, and is active in church work. She has co-authored primary social studies books for Rand, McNally and Company and served as educational consultant for Encyclopaedia Britannica Films.